THE BEST JOB EVER
Chef

Ian F. Mahaney

PowerKiDS press

New York

Published in 2015 by The Rosen Publishing Group, Inc.
29 East 21st Street, New York, NY 10010

Copyright © 2015 by The Rosen Publishing Group, Inc.

All rights reserved. No part of this book may be reproduced in any form without permission in writing from the publisher, except by a reviewer.

First Edition

Editor: Caitie McAneney
Book Design: Katelyn Londino

Photo Credits: Cover, pp. 3–24 (background design) Toria/Shutterstock.com; cover (boy) gosphotodesign/Shutterstock.com; p. 5 Echo/Cultura/Getty Images; p. 6 Bachrach/Archive Photos/Getty Images; p. 7 michaeljung/Shutterstock.com; pp. 9 (top), 14, 17 (both), 22 wavebreakmedia/Shutterstock.com; p. 9 (bottom) http://en.wikipedia.org/wiki/Culinary_Institute_of_America#mediaviewer/File:CIAGreystoneKitchens.JPG; pp. 11, 12 Monkey Business Images/Shutterstock.com; p. 13 Dmitry Kalinovsky/Shutterstock.com; p. 15 Samuel Aranda/Getty Images News/Getty Images; p. 18 Alex Wong/Hulton Archive/Getty Images; p. 19 Kzenon/Shutterstock.com; p. 21 © iStockphoto.com/Laoshi.

Library of Congress Cataloging-in-Publication Data

Mahaney, Ian F.
Chef / by Ian F. Mahaney.
p. cm. — (Best job ever)
Includes index.
ISBN 978-1-4994-0110-3 (pbk.)
ISBN 978-1-4994-0079-3 (6-pack)
ISBN 978-1-4994-0109-7 (library binding)
1. Cooks — Juvenile literature. 2. Cooking — Vocational guidance — Juvenile literature. I. Mahaney, Ian F. II. Title.
TX652.5 M34 2015
641.5—d23

Manufactured in the United States of America

CPSIA Compliance Information: Batch #CW15PK: For Further Information contact Rosen Publishing, New York, New York at 1-800-237-9932

Contents

What's Cooking?	4
A Great Job	6
Culinary School	8
Starting Out	10
Steps to the Top	12
The Executive Chef	14
Responsibilities and Perks	16
Pastry Chefs and Bakers	18
Related Jobs	20
Sweet Success	22
Glossary	23
Index	24
Websites	24

WHAT'S COOKING?

Do you like to bake pizza or fry eggs? If so, you're already a cook! A cook is someone who makes food. If you're thinking about a job when you grow up, you might think about becoming a chef.

Some people are **professional** cooks, and the best professional cooks are chefs. Chefs often work in **restaurants** and are responsible for feeding many people at once. If you're a really good chef, you can experiment with new **ingredients** and recipes. A recipe is a set of directions for making a certain dish. Good chefs make recipes that everyone wants to try.

> Do you have a favorite recipe you like to make or eat?

A GREAT JOB

Being a chef means working very hard, often for long hours. Many chefs have to work on weekends and holidays because those are busy days for restaurants. But being a chef can be a great job if you're **passionate** about food.

When you're a chef at a restaurant, you can invent new recipes that **customers** will like. Chefs think it's satisfying when customers enjoy their food. Imagine seeing a customer smile after you make the best dinner they've ever tasted. Imagine seeing your restaurant packed with customers who've heard about your cooking. That's quite an accomplishment!

CHEF BIO: JULIA CHILD

Julia Child was a famous American chef. She studied at Le Cordon Bleu, which is a world-famous cooking school in Paris. Then, she wrote a famous cookbook called Mastering the Art of French Cooking. She starred in a TV cooking show called The French Chef.

Being a chef takes a lot of creativity. You have to make a dish taste good and look good! That's called presentation.

CULINARY SCHOOL

Many cooks start their education at home by cooking for their family and friends. Some cooks start their education by working in a restaurant. Some even go to **culinary** school.

Students learn many cooking skills at culinary school. Culinary students perfect their skills for chopping vegetables and slicing fruit and meat. Students take classes that teach them how to make soups and sauces and how to combine spices in meals. Students need to exercise their senses, especially tasting, seeing, and smelling. That's not all! They also learn how to run a restaurant and make a menu.

> Many chefs get their start at the Culinary Institute of America (CIA). The CIA has locations in New York, California, Texas, and Singapore.

Culinary Institute of America at Greystone in California

STARTING OUT

Many chefs start out at a restaurant by working jobs that don't involve preparing food. They might get a job washing dishes, seating people, or serving tables. These jobs teach them about the restaurant business. If they're interested, they can apply to be a cook or go to culinary school.

After getting basic restaurant **experience**, a cook can apply for an apprenticeship. An apprenticeship is a job or special training where a person works for a professional and learns new skills. A chef's apprentice can gain important work experience in a restaurant's kitchen and show the chef their skills.

> Having experience in a kitchen gives you a better chance of becoming a chef. Unlike some other jobs, you can't learn cooking just from books. You need hands-on practice!

STEPS TO THE TOP

Restaurants commonly hire **aspiring** chefs for entry-level cooking jobs. Entry-level cooks are responsible for basic kitchen tasks. An example of an entry-level job is a prep cook, who might be in charge of cleaning and chopping vegetables. This work is called "scut work."

A line cook might be responsible for one type of cooking, such as grilling or frying.

After a prep cook proves they work hard, they may advance to be garde-manger (GAHRD–mahn-ZHAY). The garde-manger prepares smaller dishes, such as **appetizers** or salads. A garde-manger might advance to be a line cook, which is someone who makes entrées, or the main meal. This job requires more skills and experience.

THE EXECUTIVE CHEF

Very talented line cooks might have the opportunity to become a sous-chef (SOO–SHEF). The sous-chef is the second in charge of a kitchen. It's usually their goal to one day be an executive chef.

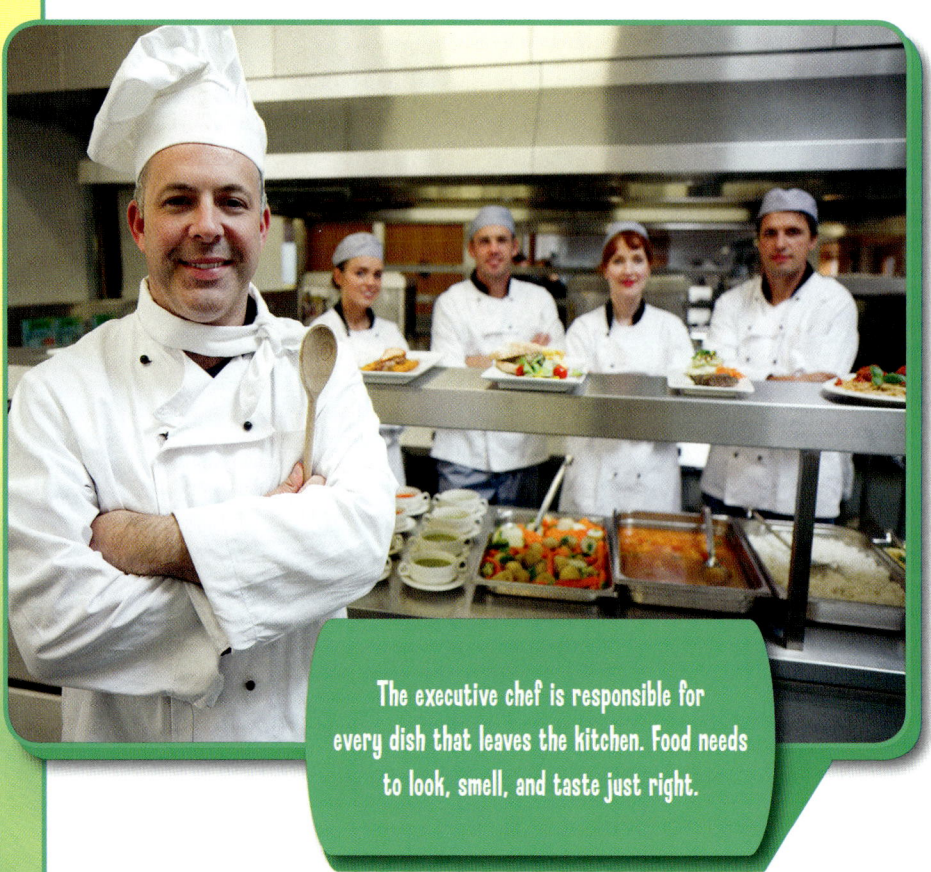

The executive chef is responsible for every dish that leaves the kitchen. Food needs to look, smell, and taste just right.

CHEF BIO: FERRAN ADRIÀ

Many think Spanish chef Ferran Adrià is the best chef in the world. He became an executive chef when he was only 23 years old. He's known for experimenting with his food, using science and creativity to make one-of-a-kind dishes.

The executive chef, or head chef, is the person in charge of the kitchen. In French, "chef" means "chief." One of an executive chef's important jobs is to **manage** the kitchen staff. The executive chef makes sure the other chefs do their jobs. Executive chefs need to be able to communicate well with their staff and teach them how to make special dishes.

RESPONSIBILITIES AND PERKS

Surprisingly, most executive chefs don't do much cooking. They're busy with other responsibilities, such as ordering repairs to kitchen tools, ordering food, and doing office work.

One responsibility most executive chefs love is creating menus. When creating a menu, the executive chef has the opportunity to experiment with new recipes. They want to create appetizers or entrées that customers will love. The sous-chef also helps the executive chef create the menu. The executive chef and sous-chef need to work together closely to manage the kitchen and make sure customers have a great eating experience.

> One perk, or benefit, of being an executive chef is the ability to make important decisions about the food. Also, executive chefs don't have to do the scut work!

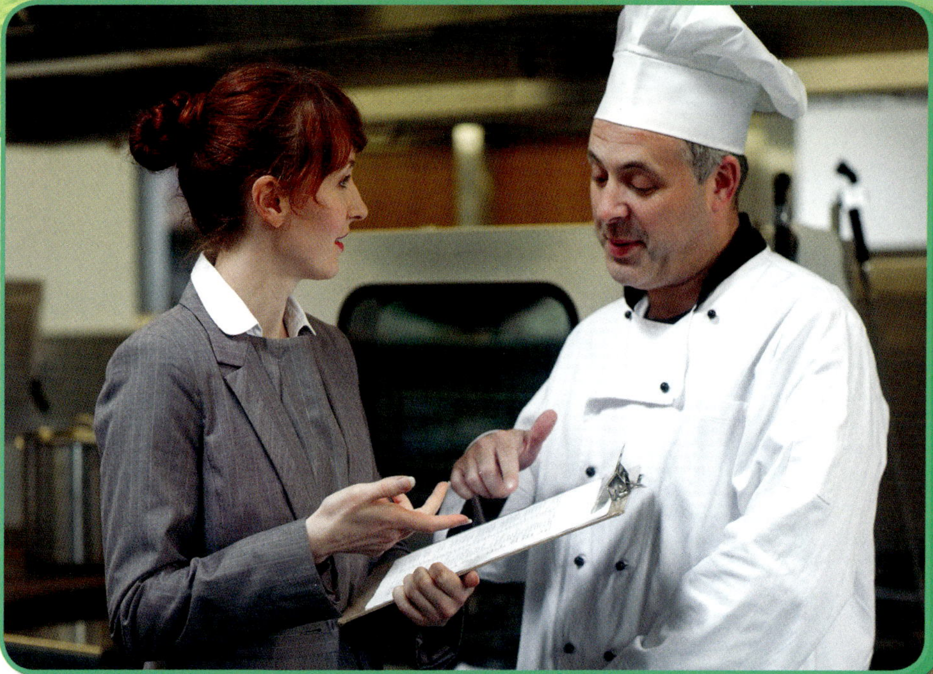

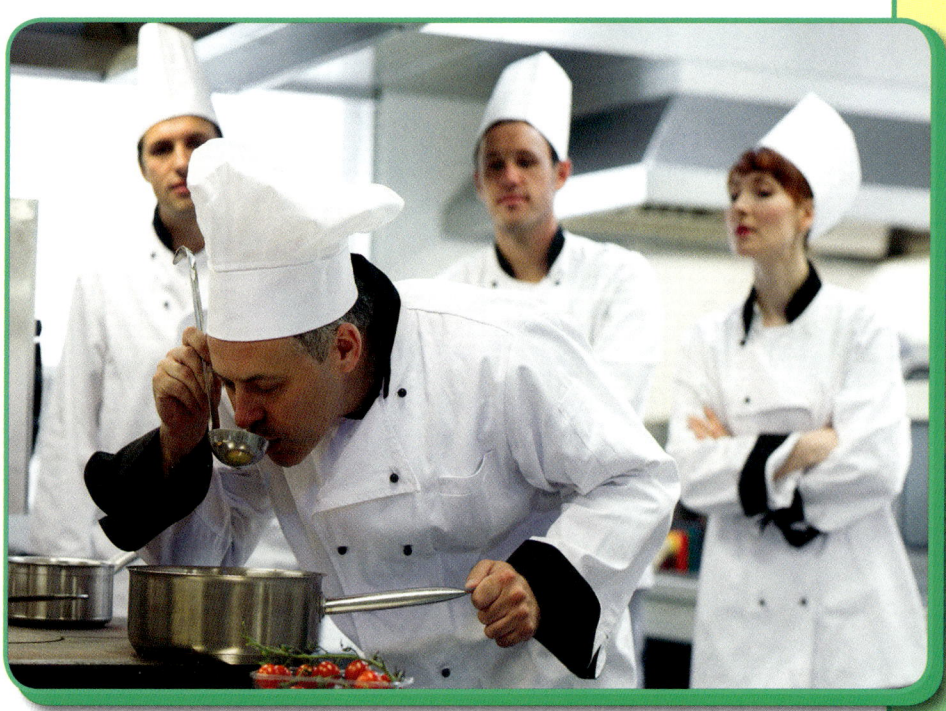

PASTRY CHEFS AND BAKERS

Bakers and pastry chefs often make the bread you eat with your meal and treats or cakes you eat for dessert. They often come to work very early in the morning. Bakers need time to make dough and let it rise into bread. Pastry chefs have to bake their treats, such as cakes, and they sometimes decorate them.

Many pastry chefs like to bake their treats from scratch, or without the help of prepared mixes. Bakers and pastry chefs often learn how to bake and decorate through work experience at a bakery. Some pastry chefs go to special culinary schools for baking.

CHEF BIO: ROLAND MESNIER

Roland Mesnier spent 25 years as the executive pastry chef for the White House. Born in France, Mesnier baked in France, Germany, England, and Bermuda. At the White House, he baked for five presidents and important guests. He never made the same dessert twice!

Some pastry chefs call themselves cake artists because they create a work of art out of cake. Some cakes look too good to eat!

RELATED JOBS

Many other jobs are related to cooking. If you love to cook, eat, and write, you might want to be a food writer. You could be a **critic** for a newspaper or magazine. Food critics eat at restaurants and then write their opinion about the food. If you like to create recipes, you can write a cookbook.

Many businesses besides restaurants make or sell food. Caterers organize the food at weddings and other parties. Food service workers and chefs work at hospitals, airlines, and schools. Can you think of other places to work if you love food and cooking?

> If you love to take pictures, you can be a food photographer. Their goal is to make people want to buy or eat the food because it looks so good.

SWEET SUCCESS

Working as a chef is a great job, but it's hard work. Chefs often work long hours standing on their feet. Sometimes they work on holidays. They're in charge of many people and have to make big decisions about the menu and the staff.

However, being a chef is fun, too! Many get to travel and learn new ways to cook. They sometimes work in restaurants all over the world. They can even own restaurants or cook on TV shows. Do you think being a chef would be a good job for you?

You may need to start from the bottom, but success as an executive chef sure is sweet!

Glossary

appetizer: A small dish that's served before the main meal.

aspiring: Strongly wanting to achieve a goal.

critic: A person who writes his or her opinion about something.

culinary: Having to do with cooking.

customer: A person who buys goods or services.

experience: Knowledge or skill gained by doing or seeing something.

ingredient: Something that goes into food.

manage: To be in charge.

passionate: Caring about something very much.

professional: Someone who is paid for what they do.

restaurant: A place where food is made and served.

Index

A
Adrià, Ferran, 15
apprenticeship, 10

B
bakers, 18

C
caterers, 20
Child, Julia, 6
critic, 20
Culinary Institute of America, 8, 9
culinary school, 8, 10, 18

E
executive chef, 14, 15, 16, 22

F
food photographer, 20
food service, 20

G
garde-manger, 13

L
line cook, 13, 14

M
Mesnier, Roland, 18

P
pastry chefs, 18, 19
prep cook, 12, 13

S
scut work, 12, 16
sous-chef, 14, 16

Websites

Due to the changing nature of Internet links, PowerKids Press has developed an online list of websites related to the subject of this book. This site is updated regularly. Please use this link to access the list: www.powerkidslinks.com/bje/chef